WHAT YOU NEED TO KNOW WHEN BUYING OR SELLING A HOME

BEFORE, DURING AND AFTER

Kari L Cross

Published by Elite Services
P.O. Box 1161
Discovery Bay, CA 94505

Email: todayseliteservices@gmail.com
Facebook: Kari Cross
Website: www.countoncross.com
Printed in the United States of America

ISBN-13: 978-0615796277
ISBN-10: 0615796273

This book is written as a reference guide to the standard California real estate process at the time of publication. This book reflects the experiences and opinions of the author and has been written as a guide of reference for the reader thinking of buying or selling a home. Readers are advised to consult a professional for specific direction on your individual real estate transaction.

DEDICATION

What You Need to Know When Buying or Selling a Home is dedicated to...

my past clients that have purchased and sold homes:
Thank you for allowing me the chance to assist you with your investments

my future clients:
I look forward to helping you through your real estate journey

buyers and sellers everywhere:
I wish you luck on your path of purchasing or selling a home.

I hope this book will bring you knowledge and direction with your next real estate transaction.

ACKNOWLEDGMENTS

To my husband Ernie, thank you for your unconditional love and support! I am so lucky to have such an amazing husband and an exceptional father to our children. You have always put the kids and I above everything else, including yourself. We make an amazing team, I am proud of the family we have created together. I can never thank you enough for being my husband and lifelong friend.

To my daughter Elyssa, her husband Nick and their daughter Lola: Elyssa, I am so proud of the women, wife and mother you have become. I am so lucky to have you as my daughter and I treasure our relationship. I am very thankful to have Nick as my son-in-law, you are an amazing addition to our family. My Princess Lola, you are a treasure! I cannot wait to experience the years to come with you and watch you grow.

To my daughter Hailey, you are the strongest person I know. You have gone through many challenges and pain over the years and handle things better than someone double your age. Going through your medical struggles has made a bond between you and I that others can't understand. You have always put 100% of yourself into anything you strive for and I am excited to see what is next for you.

To my son Hunter, you inspire me. I can't believe that at such a young age you can do the things you do. You are an amazing athlete, a caring person, and a great son and friend. I love that you work hard, care about others, and will still be silly with me.

To my parents Dennis and Linda, you have always been such great role models for me to live my life by. You are always there for my family and I; we thank you for all you have done for us over the years. The two of you have created an amazing family and I thank you for teaching me everything I know.

To my extended family, Grandpa John, Grandma Clara, Dennis, Penny, Jamie, Adam, Joshua, Justin, Jared, Cheryl, Rick, Heather, Darrian, Amanda, A. Peggy, U. Mike, Michael, Chastity, Gabriel, A. Dena, U. Lee, Keith, Luther, Lorenzo, Bob, Rhonda, Breonna, Blake, U. Johnny, Mike, Jane, Michael, Chelsea, Cheyenne, Calais: I value the close relationships I have with each of you. I have the most amazing family and I want to thank all of you for teaching me so much over the years. I have learned so much about caring for people from each of you and enjoy treating my client relationships like they are a part of our family.

To my past clients: Special thanks for choosing me as your Realtor. I am honored that you trust me to care for your best interest when buying and selling your homes.

To my friends and colleagues: Over the years I have been lucky to have many people touch my life and become valuable friends. I am thankful for the care and support I have received from my friends and colleges over the years.

To my future family members, clients, friends and colleagues, I look forward to the new relationships to come......

TABLE OF CONTENTS

SECTION 2: BUYING A HOME

SECTION 3: THE OFFER

SECTION 4: THE ESCROW

Title and escrow process begins
Lender process begins

Time Lines
Disclosures
Inspections
Appraisal
Addendums

Insurance
Good faith estimate / HUD-1
Signing documents
Loan funding
Disbursement of funds
Recording title

SECTION 5: GETTING READY TO MOVE

Get prepared to move
How to pack
Local records
Transfer services/change of address
Pack a travel kit

INTRODUCTION

Thousands of people each year read "What to expect when you're expecting." New mothers, and fathers, are excited about the birth of a new child and want to make sure they are prepared for what is to come. Being prepared for new changes in your life gives you an advantages and self-confidence to be able to experience the process free from stress and anxiety. When you know what is coming next you can enjoy the process knowing you are doing the right thing and that things are going exactly as they should.

With this thought in mind, why would someone buy or sell a home without knowing what is to come? For most people a home is the single most expensive thing they purchase in their lives. Trusting hundreds of thousands of dollars of your life savings to just anyone is a risky move, especially if you are not sure what to expect during the process. Knowing the Real Estate process will allow you to enjoy the home buying and selling experience and help relieve some of your stress and anxiety.

When you sell a home you will have many questions to insure you are making good decisions:

- **Do I need to hire a Real Estate Agent?**
- **Am I selling my home for as much as it is worth?**
- **How do I find the perfect home for me to buy?**
- **How do I make sure the paperwork is completed properly?**
- **The contract/inspections/repairs/disclosures/etc.**
- **How do I make sure I won't find myself in a lawsuit?**

Buying and Selling a home is a very exciting time and means big changes in your life. My job as a real estate agent is to make sure the process is stress free and smooth so you can have happy memories of this "big move" you are making. Most people don't move many times in their lives, let's make sure you know what to expect when you do!

This book has been written as if I was sitting with a client answering the most common real estate questions. I hope you enjoy and learn something along the way.

-Kari L Cross

SECTION 1

SELLING A HOME

There is a huge difference between buying and selling a home!

A seller is very invested in the home they are selling. They have lived in the home for many years and they have created countless memories. A seller has also purchased the home, years prior, in the hope of a large profit if the home is ever sold.

It is important that you work with people that will understand your interests in the home and can assist your needs during the process.

SHOULD I HIRE A REAL ESTATE AGENT?

Can I sell my home myself?

The answer to that question is yes. The question you should ask is, "SHOULD I sell my home myself?" The answer to that question in NO! Many people that have sold a home before, think that they could do it on their own the second time around. Some people would rather try to sell their home themselves then pay a real estate fee. Most Realtors do many things during the real estate transaction that the buyer and seller never know about. Before you decide to hire a real estate agent, you should make sure you know all they will do to help you sell your home.

An agent does not just show you some comps,

put a sign in the lawn,

wait for an offer,

and then wait for the loan to fund.

It is our job to make it look like that is all we do!

People consult professionals for many different reasons:

*   A mechanic will put a new motor and transmission in your car because they could do it in half the amount of time it might take you.

*   A doctor will operate on a family member because you want to make sure it is done correctly and your family is taken care of.

*   A fire fighter will put a home fire out quickly to save as much of your home as possible.

As you can see people hire professionals to save time, save money, and to make sure things are taken care of correctly. The fact is that hiring a professional, most of the time, will save you much more in the end than doing it yourself.

Before you decide whether or not to hire a professional to sell your home, you need to know what a real estate agent does for you during the home selling process. In most cases the money paid to a real estate agent will be much less than the money you will spend trying to sell your home yourself. In most cases, using a professional to sell your home will help your home to sell faster, save you money, and insure all paperwork is processed correctly.

REAL ESTATE ATTORNEY VS. A REAL ESTATE AGENT

In order to make sure all of the paperwork is processed correctly you will either have to hire a Real Estate Attorney, or a Real Estate Agent. Even though the attorney will be able to ensure the paperwork is processed correctly, a Realtor can provide you many more services for your money.

When you hire a real estate attorney you are only paying for assistance with paperwork. Realtors will market your home, find willing buyers, help you qualify buyers, negotiate the agreement, assist with disclosures, inspections, buyer's mortgage, escrow, etc.

COMPARE

A REAL ESTATE ATTORNEY
Charges an hourly fee (price can increase throughout the process)
Will not market your home or help to find a buyer
Only handles the paperwork for the sale
Can give advice of current laws

A REAL ESTATE AGENT
Charges a flat fee (usually a percentage of the sales price of the home)
Markets your home until a buyer is found
Handles marketing, showings, negotiation, inspections, title, lender, etc.
Can give advice on current laws, market trends and local standards

---

HIRING A REALTOR CAN ALSO MAKE YOU MONEY

As you can imagine, it takes many hours of hard work to sell a home. When you divide the number of hours spent selling a home by the cost of hiring a real estate agent, you will see this is money well spent.

Hiring a Realtor can also make you money! A Realtor has experience with negotiation and is educated on current trends, laws and markets. Without the advice of a Realtor you might accept an offer for less than the value of your home or you might sign a contract not knowing that the buyer has asked you to pay fees you are not responsible to pay.

Besides the money you can make during negotiation, selling a home incurs many out of pocket expenses. A Realtor will pay for all advertising expenses, marketing costs, signs, etc.

You can hire a Realtor to market your home <u>UNTIL IT SELLS</u>!

NO MATTER HOW MANY HOURS IT TAKES THE REALTOR!
NO MATTER HOW MUCH MONEY THE REALTOR SPENDS!

A Realtor will help you through the sale of your home for one flat rate until they complete your home selling process. You pay nothing if your home does not sell.

Hiring a Realtor can also save hours of your time! Many hours are spent showing the home to potential buyers, reviewing contracts, holding open houses, negotiating the offer, facilitating inspections, and processing lender and title paperwork.

Realtors have a huge incentive to find a buyer for your home and complete the sale as soon as possible. They use their own money on advertising and spend a lot of time marketing your home, but they only get paid if your home sales. Hiring a Realtor is free until your home is sold; they receive no money in advance for expenses.

Realtors track where most buyers come from and know how to market to those places first. Your local Realtor will be able to market your home where the buyers are most likely to see it. Simply putting a sign in your yard will only appeal to the few people that may drive by your home. In order to successfully sell your home in a timely manner, you need to make sure it is shown to as many people as possible. Marketing a home could be very costly to a seller especially if the home does not sell quickly and advertising must continue over several weeks or months.

Most Real Estate Agents pay yearly fees to several different vendors to have the capability to market your home for many weeks, at no cost to you.

- Advertise in print and on-line
- Print flyers
- Purchase signs to hold open houses
- Advertise for open houses
- Negotiate the purchase agreement
- Hire a real estate attorney to process papers
- Find a title company
- Coordinate with the title company (throughout the transaction)
- Find inspection companies
- Negotiate inspection contingencies
- Process inspections
- Coordinate with the buyer's lender
- Etc.

TIMELINES

Another reason you should hire a Realtor to help sell your home is knowledge of the transaction. After a buyer is found, the offer has been accepted and escrow is opened; the timeline process begins. During escrow your Realtor will ensure everything outlined in the contract is processed correctly. Everything has to be processed within the allotted time frame or the contract can be voided, you can be in breach, and you may be held liable.

The time line in a real estate transaction is critical!

SELLER: If papers are not signed and returned at the right time, the contract is no longer legally active. A seller can have the home held in escrow for thirty plus days and then the buyer can change their mind and decide not to buy, (with no penalty, because the paperwork was not processed correctly).

BUYER: If papers are not signed and returned at the right time, the buyer might commit to purchase the home or lose their good faith deposit. The buyer has to get all inspections completed before the inspection time expires. The loan has to be completed before the loan window closes.

The Realtors job is to manage the time lines and make sure the seller and the buyer is protected through each step. It is the Realtors job to make sure each day the paperwork gets to, or from, the right people at the right time, make sure all inspections are done, the title company gets out their papers, and the mortgage lender is ready to fund the loan on time.

The paperwork time line is another part of the process that the client should not be bothered with. Most clients don't know that Realtors are making phone calls and sending information back and forth to insure that all the correct papers are filled out properly and on time.

LEGAL PROTECTION

We live in a world were litigation is a standard practice. To sell a home to another person, you are entering into a legally binding contract with multiple parts. After you sign a purchase agreement to sell your home you also have several disclosures that have to be given to the buyer. All of these documents were implemented to alleviate litigation. Real estate agents are trained monthly on new laws and disclosures and they also have a legal team that protects them and their clients during each transaction.

When you hire a Real Estate Agent you are also hiring a legal team if any problems arise. If a buyer gets upset about something, they will sue. Regardless of whether or not they will win, you will have to undergo the stress and hassle of this on your own, or even worse, hire an attorney. Your Realtor will make sure everything is processed correctly and have all the documentation needed to assist you with any problems that can arise. Your Realtors legal team should be able to stop most problems that may occur.

EXAMPLE 1: I represented the seller on a home that was one year old. It was a standard transaction, the offer was accepted, inspections were done, and the loan funded. Two weeks after the buyer moved in I received a phone call that the outlets in the island did not work. The new owner was furious and immediately said that it was never disclosed and they were going to sue myself and the seller. Our legal department contacted the seller on my behalf to see if they had knowledge of the outlets in the island. Since the owner never lived in the home they had no idea if the outlets worked or not. The legal team found that the default was with the home inspector that did not check the island outlets. This could have been a costly fix for the original owner had he not had the assistance of my team. The legal department was able to re-direct the buyer to the home inspection company he hired that had never tested the outlets instead of the seller.

EXAMPLE 2: A seller I represented sold their home to very excited buyers. All paperwork was filed properly, the transaction closed, the buyer moved in and everyone was happy. Over a year later I received a phone call that the buyer was going to sue myself and the seller of the home. The buyer informed me that a neighbor had told them that the builder was in a class action lawsuit with other homes that were built and that the seller should have known and disclosed that. My legal team showed the buyer that the seller had no knowledge of the facts and would not be able to win. Guess what? They still filed a lawsuit. Luckily for the seller they hired a Realtor with a legal team that was able to help represent them at no cost. Everything had been properly documented and the sellers came out ahead.

As you can see from my examples, it doesn't matter if you have done the right thing throughout the transaction. If something comes up that the buyer does not like the seller will always be in trouble first. When you hire a Realtor, make sure they have legal support that will stand behind them and protect you as well. Free legal services during and after your real estate transaction is invaluable to protect yourself.

Real Estate Agents put out fires

Many of my client testimonials say the same things: "Thank you for making the home selling process so smooth." If you have ever bought or sold a home before, you may have signed a contract, maybe a counter or two, filled out some paperwork and waited to exchange keys. In fact there is so much that is done that is never brought before the buyer or seller. As a Realtor, it is my job to make sure that everything is done correctly and on time. After selling homes for many, many years, I have never had two transactions the same. Each day we have new things arise and we are able to pull from past experiences to complete each task. Sometimes problems come up that need to be brought to the client, but most fires are put out by the Realtors before the clients ever know.

CURRENT MARKET INFORMATION

The knowledge local real estate agents have on the market is very important when you are thinking about selling your home. The real estate market changes daily and knowing the condition of the market will help you decide if it is the right time to sell, how much to list your home at, what kind of offer you can expect to receive, the fees you can expect to pay, etc.

It is important know the inside knowledge of the real estate market before you put your home up for sale. This information will help you to not only price your home correctly but you will also know what other sellers, in your area, are going through.

Is it a buyer's market?

- Homes may stay on the market longer
- Seller may have to pay more fees than normal
- Seller may have to get creative on marketing
- Seller may have to do repairs on the home

Is it a seller's market?

- Home may sell quickly if priced correctly
- Seller may not have to pay some of the normal fees
- Seller may have to negotiate multiple offers
- Appraisals may come in low to stop over bidding
- Seller may be able to sell the home as-is

HOW TO FIND THE RIGHT REAL ESTATE AGENT

Picking the right real estate agent can save you money or cost you thousands of dollars. It is important that you choose the right person to handle what is probably the single largest financial investment you will ever make. You want to do everything you can to insure that things are done correctly and you get the most out of the sale of your home. You can ask several questions that will help you "hire" the right person for the job. A few questions you might want to ask:

1. **What makes you different?** What makes you unique from other Realtors? Most real estate agents copy each other and hope for results. Find what makes them different from the next. How will these differences affect you during this transaction?

2. **Why Should I list my home with you?** Where will my home be marketed? What media (newspapers, magazines, internet, etc.) does this agent advertise in? What are the Realtors views on one advertising venue versus the others?

3. **What level of service can I expect if I hire you?** Don't just ask this question, you can test it. Call a few times to ask various questions even before they come to a listing appointment. You can check how long it takes them to respond. A fast phone response is very important! If a potential buyer was driving by your home and saw the sign in the lawn they might get your Realtors phone number off the sign and call for a question. You want to make sure the Realtor you hire will get in contact with this potential buyer quickly.

4. **Get testimonials**. Realtors have, or can get, letters from their past clients. These letters will of course say that the Realtor is the best, but you can read them to find out what their strengths are. If all of the letters say "thank you for always being there" or "you made us feel comfortable" you will be able to see how this Realtor relates to their clients.

5. **Do you have an assistant, partner, or support staff?** By employing someone to handle the details of their business the Realtor can spend more time servicing your needs. You do want to make sure you are clear on how much time they will spend servicing your needs. You don't want to hire a Realtor that will then have an assistant take care of everything. It might be fine if an assistant handles the paperwork and timelines, as long as the Realtor is present for the things that are important to you during the transaction. You want to make sure you both understand what those expectations are in advance.

6. **Does the Realtor know the market?** Carefully look over the CMA provided by your Realtor that will help you decide how much your home is worth. Is the information they provide you accurate? Is it easy to understand how they arrive at the figures they have come to? Ask questions and make sure you know what the market is doing so you can make the correct decision in pricing your home.

CMA (COMPARATIVE MARKET ANALYSIS) is a term real estate agents use when they conduct and in-depth analysis of a home's worth in today's market. Most real estate agents will provide you with a CMA free of charge.

7. **What happens if you're not happy with the Realtor you hired?** Once you have entered into a contract to hire a Realtor you hope that things will go well, but that is not always the case. If you are not happy with the job your Realtor is doing, the first thing you want to do is to communicate your wants and needs to the Realtor. If your needs are still not being met, it might be time to cut your losses and move on. Most contracts lock you into working with that Realtor and can create penalties if you cancel the contract. When hiring an agent make sure you know what the penalties can be if you choose to cancel the contract. Most agents know that working with a seller that is not happy with their work is a losing situation and will release you from the contract without penalty.

HOW REAL ESTATE AGENTS FIND BUYERS

MARKETING TO OTHER REALTORS

Statistics show that most buyers find their new home after consulting with a real estate agent.

A Realtor is paid a commission from the seller of a home. A Realtor assists a buyer purchase a home at <u>NO COST</u> to the buyer. Because a buyer can use all of the knowledge and experience of a Realtor for <u>FREE</u>, every buyer uses the assistance of a Realtor to purchase a home at some point.

A seller may pay their Realtor a 6% commission

Their Realtor will give half of that commission to another Realtor that has a buyer who writes an offer and purchases the home.

LET ME SAY THAT ONE MORE TIME:
The Realtor you hire will give HALF of their money to another Realtor, just to gain access to their buyers.

If your Realtor is willing to give away half of their money to advertise to other agents, you can see why this must be very important. Every person looking to buy a home will consult with a Realtor at some point during the home buying process. Realtors that have homes for sale are willing to share their money to obtain access to these buyers. Most real estate agents have buyers that are pre-approved for a loan and are interested in purchasing a home; you need to find the one that is looking for your home.

MULTIPLE LISTING SERVICES

When you hire a Realtor they will immediately put your home on the MLS (multiple listing service) The Realtor that lists a home for sale enters in the address, age, square footage, number of bedrooms, baths, upgrades, and special notes about the home. Any real estate agent that has a buyer looking for your type of home can then make an offer to purchase your home.

> *MLS (MULTIPLE LISTING SERVICE) is a sharing of comprehensive home information among real estate professionals. Realtors enter the data about a home for sale and offer to share their commission with any Realtor who can find a buyer for the home. This online software can only be accessed by a licensed real estate agent, and it contains all the specific information about the home.*

BROKER OPEN / TOUR

Your home may also be showcased at a broker's open/tour.

> *Broker's Open/Tour is a scheduled day and time that other real estate agents can come to an open house to view the home. During this open house, agents will network about the home to find potential buyers.*

NETWORKING

Most Realtors have an additional networking system aside from the standard MLS system. With the additional networking, and broker's tours, it will ensure your home will be shown to other real estate agents several times over the period of the listing.

PRICING YOUR HOME FOR SALE

DETERMING WHAT PRICE TO LIST YOUR HOME

In the real estate industry, the concept of value is vague. The value of a house fluctuates based on the ever-changing market conditions. It is difficult to find how much a home is worth because the market changes daily.

If you have ever sold a car you know you first have to find out how much it is worth and what people are willing to pay for it. It's easy to gather the information you need to set a price from newspapers, the Blue Book, and online used car sales sites. When you gather this information you can find a price that will be attractive to potential buyers. It's very simple and it requires very little pricing expertise to sell your car. If you want to sell your home, it's not so easy and it's certainly not simple. The value of your home is much more difficult to predict and the information available to home sellers can be untrustworthy. Online home valuation sites are fun to play with, but they are based on past sales, not current factors, and they are only as good as the information entered into them. The inside knowledge that a Realtor has on the current market conditions and the homes that it is being compared to is invaluable.

Figuring out how much your home is actually worth is a tricky process. There are several "value markers" that help in determining a value. Size of the home, amenities, age, upgrades, location, views, and more, all factor into a value estimate. Checking the price of homes sold within the last 60 days that were built around the same time is the first step. You will then need to adjust for the size of the homes as well as number of bedrooms and bathrooms. Whether a home has a great view, larger lot size, backs to a busy street, etc., all becomes a factor. Once you get an estimated value from the homes that have recently sold you then need to compare that price and your home to the homes currently for sale on the market. The homes that are currently for sale will be the "competition." You want to price your home so it will sell before the other homes on the market.

THE LISTING AGREEMENT/CONTRACT

SIGNING A LISTING AGREEMENT

A listing agreement is a contract between a real estate broker (or the Realtor representative, acting in the broker's name) and the sellers of the home which gives the brokerage the right to offer the property for sale. An exclusive right-to-sell listing is the most commonly used listing agreement between a Realtor and a seller. This listing agreement gives the brokerage the exclusive right to earn a commission by representing the owner and bringing a buyer, either directly, or through a different selling brokerage who has a buyer. The owner cannot sell the property themselves without paying a commission, unless an exception is noted in the contract. This listing agreement also protects the seller's interests and ensures the Realtor must report all offers and proposals that are made on the home. The Realtor also has a fiduciary duty to represent the seller's interests. There are many parts to a listing agreement that every seller should be made aware of.

A listing agreement will consist of:

1. A beginning and ending date.
2. The price the seller wants the home to be offered for sale.
3. The amount of commission the Realtor will be paid upon sale.
4. Gives the Realtor authority to cooperate with other Realtors.
5. Authorizes the Realtor to advertise the property for sale.
6. Authorizes the Realtor to put a sign in the yard or not.
7. Authorizes the Realtor to put a lockbox on the home, or not.
8. Outlines the Realtor's obligation to advise the seller about regulations and laws that may affect the sale of the home.

SALES COMMISSION

The commission is the amount the seller is going to pay the Realtor for services rendered for the sale of the home. The commission is only paid if the home is sold, no money is paid up front and no money is paid if the home does not sell. The commission amount on both the buying and selling sides of the listing is negotiable. It is custom in most areas to pay a total 6% commission which would be 3% to the selling agent and 3% to the buying agent.

In a market with a lot of inventory and fewer buyers, (homes are selling less quickly), you might want to consider paying the selling agent the full 6% commission.

In a market with lower inventory and multiple buyers (homes are selling fast) you may be able to negotiate a small reduction in the commission amount.

A third option would be to offer the full 6% commission with a dual representation clause. With this clause you would pay a full 6% commission unless your listing agent also represents the buyer, then the commission would be lowered to an agreed upon percentage.

No money is due or paid to the Realtor until the sale of the home is complete. However, in some rare cases the seller can be responsible to pay a commission even if the home does not sell. If the Realtor provides a buyer who is ready, willing, and able to pay the full listing price (or more) for the home without contingencies and the seller changes their mind about selling their home a commission is still due. A commission is also still due if the home is in contract to be purchased by a willing, able buyer and the seller decides not to sell the home. In this last case a buyer may also be due compensation for their time wasted waiting to purchase a home that a seller refuses to sell.

Where does the commission go?

It is important to know what you are paying for.

Let's assume that a seller is hiring a Realtor and will pay a 6% commission if the home is sold. Let's also assume that the sales price of the home is $500,000, which would mean you are hiring your Realtor for $30,000. That is a large sum of money, but if you break it down, is the Realtor you hire worth it?

If a 6% commission is being paid, as we discussed previously, you can assume that 3% of that will go to the Realtor that finds a buyer for your home. This has now lowered your Realtors paycheck to $15,000. From that amount most Realtors pay a fee to their brokerage, the fee can be a flat rate of range from 20%, 30%, or 40%. Let's say your Realtor will pay 30% to their brokerage, which now leaves their commission at $10,500. Depending on your Realtors plan, the remaining money is used to pay for production and copies of custom flyers for your home, print media, internet media, open house expenses, coordination fees, signs, real estate dues, many hours of their time processing all the paperwork to sell your home, etc.

As you can see after all the expenses, you are hiring someone that specializes in their field, to handle one of your largest assets and paying them almost nothing. When you break down the number of hours Realtors spend on most transactions with their profit, most agents are highly under paid for the amount of knowledge, skill, and labor they put into selling your home.

LENGTH OF LISTING

When listing a home the Realtor spends a lot of time, effort and money to find a buyer for the home and earn a commission. To make it worthwhile for the Realtor, they want a certain minimum listing time period to have a chance of selling the home and getting paid. The listing must have an end date and it is usually three, six, or nine months. At the end of the listing period the seller can elect to re-list the property, maybe with a different listing price, with the same or new Realtor, or not list the home for sale at all. Make sure you feel comfortable with the length of the agreement and the Realtor you are going to hire.

EXPIRATION OF CONTRACT

When your listing contract expires you can elect to sign an extension to continue the contract dates and terms with the same Realtor. If you are unhappy with the Realtor you hired you may, at that time, hire a different Realtor to handle the sale of your home.

CANCELLATION OF CONTRACT

If a problem arises, will the Realtor let you cancel the agreement? Why would you want to do business with a Realtor who would not release you from the contract if you were unhappy or dissatisfied with their services? Any Realtor you hire should give you a guarantee that will let you cancel the contract if you are dissatisfied or unhappy with their services.

It is in the Realtors best interest to release an unhappy seller from their contract upon their request. If you are not happy with the Realtor you have hired to sell your home the business relationship between them and you would be strained. It is very difficult to sell a home when a seller is not working with the Realtor to make sure that everything is taken care of. It is usually in everyone's best interest to cancel the contract and move on rather than to try to work together after problems arise.

AFTER THE LISTING AGREEMENT IS SIGNED

PUTTING YOUR HOME "ON THE MARKET"

After the listing agreement has been signed by both the seller and the Realtor, the process of putting your home "on the market" will begin.

The real estate agent will put a sign in the front yard showing the neighbors and people driving by that the home is for sale. Usually a for sale sign will have a flyer box attached to it so people could get additional information on the home. The for sale sign will most likely have the real estate agents name and phone number on it so potential buyers can call for more information.

When you sign a listing agreement, you can decide whether you would like your home to appear in a multiple listing service or not. A multiple listing service (MLS) enables participating Realtors to share their listing information, and share their commission in order to give maximum exposure of your home. Putting your home on the MLS will give the home maximum exposure to multiple Realtors and also feeds to many online real estate websites. Your Realtor will enter information about the home such as number of bedrooms, bathrooms, square feet, year the home was built, and other information. Realtors are able to express additional information about the condition of the property whether it is remodeled, move in condition, needs some work, etc. Any Realtor who is a member of the local real estate board can access the homes for sale and assist their clients in finding homes that fits their wants and needs.

In addition to the MLS service provided by your Realtor, you can decide to put a lock box on your door that has a key to the home inside. Putting a lock box on your home will give other Realtors the ability to enter your home and show it to potential clients. If you decide to have a lock box put on your home, your Realtor will put special instructions in the MLS so you are comfortable with the showing arrangements. You should supply a phone number for the Realtor wanting to show the home to call to make an appointment.

In most areas a Realtor will call the seller to advise they will be going to the home at a certain time of day and will use the key in the lock box to enter the home. Make sure to give any special instructions to your Realtor such as:

Day sleeper, only show between 3pm-7pm

No showings before 10am

Weekend showings by appointment only

Cats in the home, don't let outside

Dog in back is friendly but will jump

Dog in yard, don't go in back without the owner

Alarm system code is 1234

Real estate agents belong to a board and work with a strict code of ethics. Anytime your home is shown to a potential buyer they must be accompanied by a real estate agent. With this in mind, it is always a good idea to protect yourself and remove any valuables from the home. Realtors accompany their clients through the home, but sometimes multiple clients go in multiple directions, and anything can happen. It is also highly recommended to remove any prescription medication from the bathroom cabinets. If a client needs to use the restroom, the Realtor will not accompany them. The bathroom would be the only place that cannot be watched by the Realtor.

When a Realtor calls to show the home, don't forget to "set the mood" (see section How to get your home ready for a buyer). If you are home when someone is interested in looking at the home, you should leave the house while the potential buyer views the home. Buyers take more time in a home when they are not distracted by the sellers. If the sellers are not home, buyers will look in the closets, open cabinets in the kitchen, and talk openly with their family and Realtor about things they like or dislike about the house. The more time they spend in the home and discussing different things about the home the better.

HOW TO GET YOUR HOME READY FOR A BUYER

PLAY TO YOUR HOMES STRENGTHS

Most of my sellers ask for help getting their home ready to sell. Sellers know that first impressions are important and they are anxious to do all they can to make sure their home is ready for buyers to see. The first thing you should do is try to remember what first attracted you to the home? What excited you about its most appealing features? Now that you're selling your home, you'll need to look at it as if you were buying it all over again.

If you first loved that view of the pool, make sure you leave your curtain open each time a potential buyer comes over so they can have the same first impression. If you loved the brick fireplace make sure your furniture does not block the view when people come in. Think of all the things that a potential buyer may like, and make sure they know your home provides that for them.

A spruced up house makes a great first impression on potential buyers. An attractive property grabs their attention and makes them excited about finding a house that looks and feels well-cared for. Because buyers know they'll encounter fewer problems if they buy it, your house becomes more appealing and stands out from the competition. So if you prepare your home correctly, you'll save time selling it when it's on the market.

A good first impression makes an impact on a number of levels. It's not just the way your house looks to potential buyers, but how it feels and smells to them, how their friends and family will react, how they imagine it would be to live there. Making simple improvements throughout your house can grab the attention of potential buyers and help them see why your house is right for them.

REMOVE CLUTTER

People are turned off by rooms that look and feel cluttered. Removing clutter is the number one change you can make to your home when getting ready to sell. Potential buyers are buying your house, not your furniture, so help them picture themselves and their possessions in your home by making your rooms feel large, light, and airy. As you live in your home you begin to obtain things that are not necessary for your day to day living, which should be packed away. One or two cute items for decoration is okay, but that is all you need. If your home is up for sale you are planning on moving, so let's start packing.

I show homes to potential buyers who are very interested in obtaining information about the current owner of the home. Many buyers will walk across a room to see the family pictures on the fire place mantel and they never looked at the room and won't remember that the room had a fireplace in it. Having personal belongings in a home lets the buyer think about the current owners of the home and not how their family would fit into the home. If you take a picture of your children off the wall it would be smart to replace it with a picture of a beach, forest, flowers, or something else that is general but will fill the space. Keeping decorations general will not give the potential buyer any information about who is selling the home and they can focus on looking at the features of your home instead.

Personal items should be packed away such as pictures, valuables, collectibles, books, magazines, videotapes, etc. Consider renting a storage unit to eliminate clutter in your garage as well. Simple tasks such as storing your tools and neatly rolling up your garden hose suggest that you take good care of your house. Again you want to make sure the buyer knows you take pride in your home and they will enjoy the home as much as you did.

GO ROOM TO ROOM

It is best to avoid making major renovations just to sell your home since it's not likely you will recoup those expenses from your selling price. Making minor repairs such as leaky faucets, torn screens, loose doorknobs, and broken windows may however help you obtain the price you are looking for. Make sure any repairs you do are done well, buyers won't take you seriously if your home improvement efforts look messy or unfinished.

The kitchen is the most important room for most buyers. Make sure your kitchen looks inviting and is clutter free. Small countertop appliances should be placed in cabinets and not left on the counters. If the counters are empty potential buyers will be able to visualize their items in the kitchen. Wood cabinets can be polished to give an added shine. Counters with grout can be cleaned and sealed to give a fresh new look. Make sure the garbage is dumped daily so no unwanted smells will come from the kitchen.

Don't forget the bathrooms! It is important to make sure the mirrors are cleaned, and that chrome and porcelain surfaces sparkle. Look at the shower and bath, anything that does not sparkle should get your attention. Make sure the garbage is dumped and the toilet paper roll is not empty. New towels laid out will give an inviting feeling for a low cost.

Check the condition of your carpet, sometimes a professional carpet cleaner is a great way to spruce up the look of the home. If your carpet is really old and worn you can consider replacing it with a light neutral color. If you don't want to replace it, you can suggest to potential buyers that you are willing to provide a small credit for them to purchase carpet after escrow. This will give a potential buyer the feeling that they are getting an additional deal on your home.

Storing clothes you won't soon use will make your closets look more spacious. Doors should open and close easily and shelves and racks should be in order. Make sure your shoes and clothes are neatly arranged so that buyers can see how large your closet is not a mess.

Clean any soot out of the fireplace. Remove any smoke damage on the wall surrounding the fireplace. If you have a wood burning fireplace, putting new logs in the fireplace will look inviting and ready for a comfortable afternoon fire.

In general, if you intend on painting the interior of your home, light neutral colors will appeal to most people and will make rooms look larger.

Look around the outside of your home as well. You can spruce up your garden and lawn by trimming shrubs and replace any dead plants. Trying to add some color to the yard will help the home look more inviting. Ensure the house numbers, mailbox and exterior lighting are in good condition. Repair loose trim, drain pipes and fencing. The driveway and entryway need to be free from clutter. The yard and patio should be neat and outdoor furniture must be clean and in good shape.

SET THE MOOD

When a potential buyer is on their way to your home, make sure you "set the mood" for them as soon as they walk into the house. Whether it is the late evening, or the middle of the afternoon, you should turn on every light in the house and open every window. The most important thing you can do is get as much light into your home as you can. Turning on the lights and opening the windows even in the middle of the day will give your home a light large feel. Just make sure that you have no burned out light bulbs and all of the light fixtures and windows have been cleaned.

You can set the kitchen table with some colorful placemats, nice dishes, cloth napkins, fancy glasses, and a center piece. This inviting setting will give a potential buyer the feel that they will want to sit down in your kitchen and have dinner. If you have recently baked cookies, the smell will fill the house and you can put them on the counter to help with the "dinner is ready" feeling.

Play some music. While a potential buyer walks through your home having some low, soft music playing in the background will have a soothing feeling. While listening to the sound of music playing, the buyer will get a feeling that you care about how they feel in your home and you want them to love your home as much as you do.

If you have an older bathroom adding towels and accent items to the bathrooms may distract a buyer from the age of the bathroom fixtures, tile, etc. Place some neutral smelling scents in a decorative dish on the back of the toilet to give a nice aroma.

Think about when you walk through a model home. The way the house is staged as if your family was actually currently living in the home. They may have a board game laid out on the table in the loft but the rest would be very simple. A bed, dresser, lamp and two pictures on a wall are all that is needed in a bedroom. Keep in mind your home is not a model home, you actually have to live in your home as you are trying to sell it. Keep the things you may need day to day, but try to remove any other items that you enjoy but don't need on a daily basis.

DON'T FORGET THE OUTSIDE

The front and back of the home is just as important as the inside. How the home looks from the street and the type of entertaining the new owners can do in the back is important.

When a potential buyer arrives at your home make sure the lawn is mowed, leaves are picked up and the weeds are pulled. Showing care in the outside of your home shows the potential buyer that you have also cared for the inside of the home.

You want to do the same in the back yard. If you can make the back yard look clean and inviting the buyer will be able to think about how nice it will be to entertain family and friends in the yard.

WHAT IF MY HOME <u>DOESN'T</u> SELL RIGHT AWAY?

Sometimes when a home is listed and put on the market it doesn't sell right away. This could be for several different reasons... the home is priced to high, the condition of the home has an impact on buyer opinion, market values changed since the home was listed, other homes on the market changed since your home was listed, etc.

COMMUNICATION

<u>Weekly:</u> It is important to have a lot of communication with your Realtor during the listing period so you can be informed and not frustrated. Your Realtor should contact you weekly with updates on showings and feedback of your home. Even if there is nothing to report, that is information that you need to be aware of.

<u>Monthly:</u> Each month it is a good idea to do a new CMA on your home so you can be aware of how the market has changed in the last 30 days and what that impact may have on your home. Sometimes additional comparable homes come on the market at a lower price that will impact the sale of your home. If this happens you may consider a price reduction of your home to stay on track with the market.

<u>COMMON MISTAKE:</u> Many sellers list their home for sale and are unaware of what is happening in the market until 6 months later when they are questioning why their home is not selling. A small price reduction earlier in the process may save you a large price reduction later in the process.

NOTES

SECTION 2

BUYING A HOME

If you are a first time home buyer, you are thinking about one of the largest purchases of your life. The home buying process can seem overwhelming but when you are informed and use a qualified team of professionals you will feel more comfortable during the process.

If you have purchased a home before, make sure you get the correct information on the current market and laws that have changed since your last purchase. I have been selling real estate for many years and no two transactions have ever been the same.

WHERE DO I BEGIN?

HOW DO I KNOW WHEN I AM READY

Whether you are a first time home buyer, looking to purchase a second home, or a retirement home, the first step is to know when you are ready. Being ready to make a move is important, but many things need to fall in line to have a smooth home buying experience.

So many variables and questions need to be answered to see if it is the right time to move. You need to find a Realtor, find a lender, and get prequalified for a home mortgage. Once you know how much you qualify for, you can continue in the process. After you are prequalified you will be able to search different neighborhoods to see what type of home you can purchase in your price range. It is then that you can decide if it is the right time to move into a new home.

If you don't know a lender, your Realtor is the best source for advice on the perfect lender to choose for your needs. It is important to choose a lender that will be able to successfully process your paperwork and provide you with a mortgage on the home you are purchasing. Your Realtor knows what local lenders are easy to work with and can help you decide if you are ready to buy a home.

FINDING A REALTOR

Real estate agents help a buyer find a new home at NO COST to the buyer! All fees to the real estate agent are paid by the seller. A real estate agent can help you find a home, write a contract, obtain inspections on the home, facilitate title, and more, and it will cost you nothing.

When you call a real estate agent you should ask a few questions to make sure they will be able to assist you with your needs. You will want to know if they specialize in the areas you are looking in for a home, how long they have been selling real estate, etc.

Find out if the real estate agent can e-mail you homes that are for sale in your price range. It is important to start gathering information about your local area a few month before you are ready to buy a home. Even if you are not quite ready to purchase a home, it is a good idea to have a real estate agent send you homes you may be interested in each week so you will be able to watch the market until you are ready.

BUYER BROKER AGREEMENT

When you find the Realtor you want to work with you will sign a Buyer Broker Agreement (also called a Buyer's Agency Form). This form is very important to both the Realtor and the buyer.

When a buyer signs this agreement, they are committing to working with that Realtor exclusively. The buyer is agreeing to use the Realtors services exclusively, and agrees to allow the Realtor to work on the buyer's behalf during the entire transaction.

When a Realtor signs this agreement they are committing to provide the buyer with a high standard of care. The Realtor is legally committing to work on the buyers behalf and to have their best interest during the entire transaction. The Realtor may not disclose your personal information or intentions to others without your consent.

As you can see the Buyer Broker Agreement is important for the Realtor, but it is also very important to protect the buyer at the same time.

If after you sign this form you are unsatisfied with the Realtor you are working with you have to notify them of your desire to cancel the agreement. You should send an email or a letter to them and ask for an immediate response in writing so you will have a record that they were notified. You cannot work with a different Realtor until the first Realtor acknowledges your right to cancel the agreement. If you are unable to get a response from the Realtor you can contact their broker and ask them for a confirmation of cancelation.

WHAT IS A HOME MORTGAGE

A Mortgage is a loan secured by a lien on real estate. A loan made for the purpose of purchasing, building or rehabilitating real property, and secured by that property. The term mortgage is also used to describe a promissory note of debt, which includes the terms of the debt's repayment. Many different types of loans are available and it is important to look at all of your options so you will be able to make an educated decision about which loan would be best for you.

Some loans are privately insured and some are federally insured. Conventional loans are not government insured and have fewer specific restrictions. You may also want to consider mortgage loans backed by a federal agency such as the Federal Housing Administration (FHA loans) or the Department of Veterans Affairs (VA loans). Insured mortgages such as FHA and VA loans may be more attractive than conventional mortgages in some ways such as offering lower down payment requirements. It is important however to know that these loans may only be available for certain kinds of homes or for properties whose value is below a specified price.

The interest rate is important and will affect your monthly payments. Some mortgage loans may have a fixed rate mortgage (rates that will stay fixed for the life of the loan), adjustable rate mortgages or ARMs (rate that may change), or a convertible mortgage (a combination of fixed and variable rates). In some cases the amount of the down payment will influence the interest rate that you pay (the larger the down payment, the lower the interest rate). The interest rate directly affects your monthly mortgage payment. Keep in mind if you opt for an adjustable rate mortgage your monthly payment will change per the terms of the loan.

Make sure you are aware of the length of the loan. Having a 15, 30, or 40 year loan will affect your monthly payment as well. If you receive a 15 year loan your payment will be much higher than stretching the payments out over 30 years.

Know if your loan has a pre-payment penalty clause. Some loans will charge you a penalty if you re-finance or pay off your loan within the first few years.

Another option you will need to consider is paying your property taxes and home insurance, as an impound, in your monthly payment. You can opt to pay your tax and insurance bill in a lump sum annually as the bill comes in, or you can pay smaller amounts with your mortgage each month. Make sure you ask how much your monthly mortgage payment would be and then compare that with your taxes and insurance impounded in the payment.

Make sure you ask your lender how one loan differs from another and how different features of the loan will affect your mortgage.

THE THREE MORTGAGE STEPS

STEP 1, PREQUALIFICATION: This is the process where the lender will look at a basic copy of your credit report and uses information provided by you to determine how much mortgage you can afford simply based on your income. No accounts or employment is verified. Once you have the basic numbers of what you qualify for and how much your monthly payments would be, you can begin to start looking for a home.

STEP 2, PREAPPROVAL: While you are looking for a home to purchase, your mortgage lender will be working on obtaining preapproval of your loan. They will need paperwork from you including bank statements, proof of employment, etc. Once the mortgage lender verifies your credit and employment your mortgage is approved, subject to appraisal of the property you choose to buy.

STEP 3, FINAL LOAN APPROVAL: Final approval occurs when the property has been appraised, all documentation is in the hands of the lender and all contingencies have been met.

WHY GET PRE-APPROVED IN THE BEGINNING?

It is important to call a mortgage lender and start the preapproval process if you are thinking of buying a home. The best way to find a great mortgage lender is to ask friends, family members, co-workers, or your real estate agent for their recommendations. You will feel more at ease if you are working with someone that you know is recommended by someone you trust. Getting preapproved for a home loan prior to looking for a home will be beneficial to you, your Agent, and the seller.

THE BUYER: You will have valuable information to help you find a new home. Many questions need to be answered when you are looking for a home mortgage. It is important to answer these questions in the beginning of the home buying process. It is fairly simple to start a mortgage prequalification and it will put you on course to finding a great new home.

THE REAL ESTATE AGENT will know your financial parameters and can find a home that will fit your specific situation. Being preapproved will save you time because you won't be looking for homes outside your price range. It is also important for your Realtor to communicate with your mortgage lender. In some cases a buyer will not qualify for a loan unless closing costs are paid by the seller, and some loans don't allow any credits from the seller. Knowing your loan information up front will allow you to look at homes that will fit into your criteria.

THE SELLER is looking to sell their home as quickly and smoothly as possible. If you are able to write an offer with a prequalified loan, it would be a much stronger offer than someone writing an offer that is not prequalified for a loan. Even if the unqualified offer is a little higher than your offer, most sellers will opt for the offer that is already approved. When you do find your dream home, making a complete offer helps your chances of having the seller accept your offer.

HOW MUCH CAN I REALLY AFFORD?

Getting preapproved will give you the maximum dollar amount you qualify to purchase a home, but it's up to you to decide what you can afford. It is important to consider your monthly bills and income to determine what is a comfortable mortgage for you. Many times my clients are approved for more than they can comfortably afford and they opt to purchase a home for a little less than their qualification amount.

CLOSING COSTS AND FEES:

Another important thing to be aware of is closing costs and fees to purchase a home. As a buyer you will be responsible for several different fees. Closing fees will range from mortgage costs, and appraisal fee, to title insurance, home insurance, taxes, and notary fees. These fees will be charged in addition to your down payment. Depending on the type of loan and your location, closing costs can range from 2-5% of the mortgage amount. Some buyers are unable to pay the additional money upfront and they use a credit from the seller to cover the fees and closing costs, this will depend on the type of loan you receive.

MOVE IN COSTS:

You should also have extra money set aside for costs after you move into your new home. Most homes will have, at minimum, a list of "honey do" items that should be taken care of after you purchase the home. Don't forget about costs to purchase window coverings, paint, carpet, or landscaping. Even if the home is in "move in condition" unexpected things still come up. Extra money can also be used for new furniture or decorations in your new home.

FINDING THE RIGHT HOME

When you are serious about buying a home, it is important to look at a few homes with your real estate agent. An agent will be able to better assist you find your dream home after they walk through a few homes with you. It is important to walk through the homes and let your agent know everything you like and don't like about the house.

Buyers remember to tell their real estate agents how many bedrooms they need, the size of the home, number of bathrooms, or if they would like a pool. When a buyer is looking at a home they remember other things that may also be important to them like whether they would like the kitchen to have an island, they may need two sinks in the master bathroom, they might want to have side yard access, or they may need to have a separate family room and living room. As a buyer locates things they like and don't like in each home, they can let the real estate agent know how important it is that the home has or does not have each feature. The real estate agent will have more information to help find only homes that have all of the wants and needs of the buyer. This will save the buyer time looking at homes that will definitely not work for them.

Now that your real estate agent knows what you are looking for, it is only a matter of time before you find your dream home. When you do find a home you like, make sure you drive through the neighborhood both during the day and in the evening hours so you can get a sense of the community. If you are moving to a new town you should drive from the new home to your work place during your normal commute hours. Some buyers find a new home during the weekend and they are not aware how long it will take them to get to their job in the morning, or get home in the evening.

Don't forget you are not only buying a home you love, you want to make sure you love the neighborhood, the town, the people in the community, etc.

NOTES

SECTION 3

THE OFFER

When negotiating an offer you need to know some of the important parts of the contract that will affect the sale/purchase for both yourself and the other party.

If you are the buyer writing an offer to purchase your dream home, or the seller looking at an offer, many factors have to be addressed.

Some of the terms on the contract are non-negotiable for either the buyer or the seller to allow the transaction to be complete. It is important for both parties to determine which factors are wants and which are needs so they can negotiate the terms of the contract correctly.

BUYER

WRITING THE OFFER

When you find a home that fits all your needs, you are ready to write an offer. Your Realtor will have to work with you and your lender to write an offer. Your Realtor will first have to speak with your lender to find out what kind of loan you qualify for. All loans have different regulations and it is important that the contract is written correctly. Once your Realtor knows what your restrictions are they can help you decide how to write the best offer. Some loans specify that the buyer or seller must pay certain fees. Some loans allow the buyer to receive a credit towards closing costs but it is limited to the amount of credit they are allowed to receive. The length of escrow may also be affected because some loans will need a longer time of escrow to ensure the loan will fund on time.

SELLER

READING THE OFFER

When a potential buyer writes an offer on your home, many things should be looked at to analyze if the offer should be accepted or not. You cannot just look at the price offered and say I will take it. Realtors have experience reading and negotiating and they can show you all of the hidden factors in the offer and make sure you sell your home for top dollar. Is the buyer asking for any credits from the seller? Is the buyer asking the seller to pay for fees typically paid by the buyer? Is the financing strong? Will the lender be able to fund the loan as it is written in the contract? These are just a few of the questions that Realtors help clients answer when deciding to accept an offer or to write a counter. A good Realtor can navigate through the purchase contract and help you to decide what offers may need to be countered to protect you from hidden fees.

THE CONTRACT

PURCHASE PRICE

The first thing that everyone looks at is the price offered for the home. Although this is very important, it is only important when we factor in all of the other terms of the offer as well. The offer price minus credits and closing costs is the actual amount being offered on the home.

SELLER: As a seller it is important to make sure you know what your bottom line will be when accepting an offer. Some sellers may want to choose the offer with the highest dollar amount but that offer may not net the seller as much as an offer with a lower dollar amount. A buyer can ask the seller to pay for items usually paid by a buyer, or they may ask the seller to pay a closing cost credit, etc. Your Realtor can advise what fees are customary for the seller to pay and what might be an added expense for you if you accept the offer.

BUYER: As a buyer it is important to know what kind of market you are purchasing a home in. If it is a buyer's market you can be aggressive and ask the seller to pay for some of the buyer fees. If it is a seller's market and the seller is receiving many offers you have to work hard to make your offer better than the others. You may want to pay some of the seller's fees and change other terms on the contract to make your offer stand out.

CLOSE OF ESCROW DATE

COE (Close of Escrow) is the second thing to look at on the contract. This is an important time frame that is sometimes overlooked. The length of escrow is important to both the buyer and the seller for different reasons.

SELLER: Most sellers want a very short escrow period to ensure that everything is processed quickly and that no problems arise. Some buyers are unable to close quickly because of the type of loan they are getting on the home or the inability to move quickly. If you know what the buyer's situation is, it can help you make an informed decision when accepting offers.

BUYER: For some buyers the length of escrow is not in their control. Depending on the type of loan the buyer qualifiers for may depend on the length of escrow needed to process that loan. Lenders may need a minimum of 45 days to fund your loan. If you are held to a longer escrow period make sure you let the seller know that is the only reason for the long escrow and that you can negotiate other factors on the offer to make it more appealing to the seller.

FINANCING INFORMATION

The buyer has to inform the seller of the type of financing they will be using to purchase the home. The seller will review the financing information along with a letter from the buyer's lender to determine if the loan is a high or low risk of funding on time. The seller is looking for an offer that gives them the amount of money they need, in the shortest amount of time, with the least amount of risk. Is it an all cash offer? Is it a conventional loan, FHA, or VA loan? Is it 100% financing, 10% down, 20% down, etc?

GOOD FAITH DEPOSIT

The potential buyer will provide a "good faith deposit." This deposit usually comes in the form of a check made out to the title company. This money is entered into escrow and held as a security that the buyer will do everything possible to purchase the home.

A larger deposit might make a seller feel more at ease and secure that the potential buyer will do all they can to insure the home will close escrow.

SELLER: If one buyer offers a good faith deposit of $1,000 and a second buyer offers a deposit of $5,000, you might think the second buyer is less of a risk than the first buyer. You might want to find out if the buyer is able to increase their deposit either at the time of the offer or soon after. Some buyers might be better qualified but they may have to move their money from a different account before they are able to increase the deposit.

BUYER: As a buyer giving a larger down payment shows the seller that you are ready to purchase a home. The deposit is held in escrow and becomes part of your down payment at the end of the escrow transaction. If you find something wrong with the home and decide not to purchase the home within your contingency period you get your full deposit back. The seller can keep this deposit if you have removed all contingencies and you don't buy the home in the end. Make sure your Realtor explains this process to you in detail.

CONTINGENCY PERIOD

The contract has many different time sensitive sections. Until all of these time frames have been met, the buyer has rights to review the home and their loan and decide if they can/will purchase the home. The sooner the buyer removes contingencies of inspections, appraisal, and loan the sooner the seller will know that the buyer will guarantee the purchase of the home.

> *CONTINGENCY PERIOD is an allotted time designed to serve three major purposes for a home buyer. It allows time for the buyer to inspect the property, have the home appraised, and get loan approval ready.*

SELLER: The best offer for a seller is when the buyer has no loan contingency, no appraisal contingency, and is buying the home as-is with no inspection contingency. Even with a cash buyer, most buyers will want time to inspect the home and ensure that they know exactly what they are about to purchase. If a buyer needs a loan, appraisal and/or inspection period, it benefits the seller if the length of time is shortened as much as possible.

BUYER: In most areas a buyer has 17 days to get all inspections on the home and review all disclosures. To make your offer more appealing you can plan for a 7-10 day inspection period. Any of the three contingencies (loan, appraisal, or inspection) that can be shorten will show the seller that you are doing everything possible to purchase the home.

CREDITS

Many buyers need to ask the seller to help pay some of their closing costs by asking for a credit. The buyer may also ask for a credit to purchase new carpets, do repairs to the home, etc. The seller will need to factor these credit amounts into the asking price to determine their bottom line.

SELLER: It is important for the seller to determine if the credit is a want or a need for the buyer. Some buyers are unable to purchase the home without a closing cost credit. If this is the case, you may want to assist the buyer with a closing cost credit but increase the purchase price to cover that added expense. If you can do this, you will be giving the buyer the credit they need and still getting the same amount of money for the home that you are looking for.

BUYER: When you are asking the seller for a credit it is a good idea to explain to the seller why you want/need the credit. If you have to have a credit to purchase the home, you want to make sure that the seller does everything they can to provide that credit. If you are asking for a carpet credit, make sure the seller knows that you would like to put new carpet in the home and maybe they would be willing to not give a credit for that or replace the carpet for you instead.

CONTINGENT / NON-CONTINGENT

Is the offer contingent or non-contingent? Some buyers have to sell another home before they can purchase a home. Sometimes a buyer has to sell another piece of property before they qualify for the loan to purchase a home. If an offer is contingent on the sale of a home, many questions will need to be addressed.

SELLER: If a buyer has to sell another home before they are able to purchase your home, you will want to find the answers to several different questions to determine if it is a strong offer. Your Realtor can help you determine what stage the contingency is at so you can determine the risk in accepting the offer.

BUYER: If you are writing an offer contingent on the sale of another home, you should provide the seller with the answers to all the questions above so they can decide if they want to accept your offer. Most sellers are scared to accept a contingent offer, but if they are informed with the correct information they might see the risk is not as high as they thought.

A FEW QUESTIONS:

- Is the home already up for sale?
- Is the home already in escrow?
- When is the home supposed to close?
- What kind of financing did their buyer use to purchase that home?
- Have all contingencies been removed on that home?

TERMITE INSPECTIONS

TERMITE: The contract will have a section allocated to the termite inspection of the home. It will be marked who is to pay for the inspection, who will pay for Section 1 repairs and who will pay for any Section 2 repairs.

> **SECTION 1 REPAIRS:** *Any active infestation or dry rot.*
>
> **SECTION 2 REPAIRS:** *Things that can be potential problems at a later date if not taken care of soon.*

SELLER: The seller will want to know if the buyer is requesting a termite inspection and who is responsible to pay for the inspection as well as any problems that may be found. If you are asked to pay for Section 1 repairs, it is a good idea to put a cap on the amount of work you are willing to pay for. You don't want to agree to pay for this expense and then find that there is a huge problem under the house that will cost you several thousands of dollars. Putting a cap on the amount you are willing to pay for will allow you the option to renegotiate if the inspection finds a lot of damage instead of locking you into what can be an unknown expense.

> ### EXAMPLE OF SELLER OPTIONS WITH A FEE CAP
>
> If you put a $1,000 cap on expenses and the report comes back and says you have $4,000 of damage, you will have options.
>
> Option 1: You can agree to pay the $4,000 and continue with the sale of the home.
>
> Option 2: You can ask the seller to pay for part of the repairs.
>
> Option 3: Cancel the contract and put the home back on the market to try to find a buyer willing to purchase the home with the repairs made. You will have to advise the next buyer about the damage and ask them to purchase the home as-is.

BUYER: If the buyer asks for a termite inspection, most loans will require all Section 1 work to be repaired before the loan can be funded. Make sure you know who is responsible to pay for the Section 1 repairs in advance.

OTHER INSPECTIONS

The contract has a section for the buyer to advise what other inspections they may be getting on the home and who will pay for each of these inspections. The buyer should advise the owner of all known inspections, but can obtain additional inspections later as well. In most cases the buyer will pay for a home inspection and the home inspection may find something that requires the buyer to obtain an additional inspection. At that time the buyer can add a pool inspection, roof inspection, etc.

ZONE DISCLOSURE REPORT

A Zone Disclosure report (or Natural Hazard Disclosure) is a form that assists sellers in their legal obligation to inform buyers of potential hazards in the area around the home. This includes, but is not limited to: earthquake zone, flood zone, airport influences, Megan's law, toxic mold act, mello-roos, environmental contamination sites, etc. The zone disclosure report must be purchased and supplied to the potential buyer. Make sure it is specified what company will be providing the report and who is responsible to pay for it.

ESCROW, TAX AND OTHER FEES

Each state, county, or city has different customary fees that should be paid by the buyer or seller, but all fees are negotiable. These fees might be escrow fees, owner's title insurance policy, county transfer tax, city transfer tax, HOA transfer fee, HOA document preparation fees, home warranty, etc. All of these fees can add up and it is important you are aware of which fees you will be responsible to pay for. Know what fees you are usually responsible to pay for and which fees are being paid for you by the other side.

FIXTURES

Make sure both the buyer and seller understand what items are included or excluded in the sale. Some sellers might want to take items from the home that by law are required to stay in the home. Having a clear list of items to stay in the home and items that will be removed from the home will help to make sure both the buyer and seller have appropriate expectations.

SELLER: As a seller you can take the things you would like as long as both parties agree. If the buyer wrote an offer on the home and you intend to take the dining room light fixture and replace it with a different one, you need to make sure the buyer understands that the light fixture they saw in the home will be removed. Make sure you put in writing and have the buyer acknowledge that the light fixture will be different than the one they saw in the home.

BUYER: The lawn furniture in the back yard is the property of the seller and does not stay with the home, but you can ask the seller to include the furniture with the sale of the home. It is important to talk to your Realtor so you know what items in the home will stay and which items you want to ask the seller to leave behind for you.

COUNTER OFFERS

Once the seller looks at all of the terms of an offer they can either accept the offer just as it is written, or give the potential buyer a counter offer of terms they want changed on the contract. The potential buyer will look at a counter offer from the seller and decide to either accept the counter offer or give the seller another counter offer. The counter offers can continue to go back and forth until an agreement is reached or one party decides not to continue with the transaction.

In some cases a seller might receive more than one offer on their home. If multiple offers are received the seller may provide all of the potential buyers with counter offers. The seller must put in writing that multiple offers were received on the home and multiple counter offers are being presented. If more than one counter offer is accepted the seller will have to take all of the above terms into consideration and decide which one nets them the most money and which one will have a better chance in funding the loan.

When writing a counter offer it is important to know as much information as you can so you will be able to make a counter offer that will work for both parties. If you can separate needs vs. wants of the person on the other side of the contract, as discussed in the previous section, it will save you a lot of time and might allow you to come out with more in your favor in the end. It is important not to ask for something that the buyer/seller is unable to change because of loan needs, and instead ask for changes in other areas that will still get you the bottom line you are looking for. Your Realtor will help you determine different ways to reach the same results that may work best for both buyer and seller.

EXAMPLE 1: If the buyer does not have enough money to pay for closing costs, they may ask the seller to pay $10,000 towards the buyers' fees. If the seller is not willing to net $10,000 less for the home, they may choose to raise the purchase price of the home $10,000 so they can give the buyer the credit they need to purchase the home. This will net you the same amount of money and work for the buyer as well as the seller.

EXAMPLE 2: If the buyer's lender will not allow them to purchase a home with any section 1 damage they may ask the seller to pay for all section 1 repairs. The seller should put a cap on the amount they will provide for repairs. If the repairs required are higher than indicated on the offer, the seller can choose to raise the amount they are willing to pay, they may ask the buyer to pay the difference, or the seller can opt not to sell the home.

As you can see there are many different scenarios as to how buyers and sellers may benefit from the sale and purchase of a home. Bringing all of the different aspects of the home together can sometimes take a little negotiation. Once both parties agree on all of the terms and everything is signed, it is time to open escrow.

NOTES

SECTION 4

THE ESCROW PROCESS

Once all the negotiating is finished and all the terms of the sale have been worked out, the home sale/purchase officially begins and it is time to "Open Escrow. There are three major steps in the escrow process.

ESCROW is when the financial dealings of two parties in an agreement Is monitored by an independent third party known as an escrow agent. The escrow agent ensures that all terms of the contract have been fulfilled correctly and then they release the funds in accordance with the guidelines established in the contract.

STEP 1: Open Escrow account and start the loan process

STEP 2: Time Lines, Disclosures, Inspections, Appraisal, Addendums

STEP 3: Insurance, Loan Funding, Sign Docs, HUD, Record New Title

ESCROW
STEP 1

ESCROW ACCOUNT OPENED

BUYER: The buyer's Realtor will give a copy of the signed offer to the title company agreed upon. Along with the offer, the title company will be given the good faith deposit check to cash and hold in an escrow account until the close of escrow date. The title company will process paperwork such as preliminary title report to give to the buyer to review. The title company will contact the buyer to determine how the new owners want to hold title. There are many different ways to hold title in a home, but the most common might be: Sole Ownership (one buyer), Tenants in Common (two unmarried partners, equal or un-equal), Joint Tenancy (equal ownership), or Community Property (can only be a husband and wife.) The title representative will advise the buyer of the different title options so you can choose the best fit for your needs.

TITLE COMPANY: It is the job of the title company to handle all the funds with the sale and purchase of a home and ensure the buyer receives a clean title on the home. The title company will receive all of the bills needed to be paid by both the buyer and seller, such as; taxes, insurance, loan fees, real estate fees, inspection costs, etc. The title company will obtain the money from the buyer's mortgage lender and ensure that the seller's mortgage loans are paid as well as disbursing all other fees. Paperwork will be processed by the title company in preparation for the change in ownership. The title company will also make sure that all liens are cleared on the title and that the new owners are recorded correctly on the deed.

SELLER: The title company will contact the seller to get all of the current mortgage information on the home. They can coordinate with another title company if the seller is purchasing another home to help with a smooth transition.

THE LOAN PROCESS BEGINS

The buyer's real estate agent will give a copy of the signed offer to the buyer's mortgage lender. The lender will start loan papers as well as order an appraisal of the home. While the mortgage lender waits for the appraisal to be complete, the buyer will provide the lender bank records, employment verification, and any other paperwork needed to complete the loan package. The mortgage lender will create a loan package of the buyer's information and try to sell it to a financial institution that will carry the loan on the home.

ESCROW
STEP 2

TIME LINES

It is very important that both the buyer's and the seller's real estate agents are aware of all the different time periods outlined in the contract. The time periods are a crucial part of the contract and it is important that things are completed before the time frames run out. All of the contingency periods have pre-set time frames, but they can be negotiated if needed.

A contract may say that the seller only has 7 days to give the buyer disclosures, the buyer might only have 17 days to complete all inspections on the home, the buyer may only have 3 days to review disclosures after they are received, or the buyer may only have 17 days to remove loan contingency, and so on.

EXAMPLE 1: The buyer will have to obtain all of their inspections on the home and ask for any repairs to be made before the 17th day. If the buyer asks for repairs on the 18th day, the seller will not have to accommodate any requests and the buyer will be locked into buying the home as-is.

EXAMPLE 2: When a Realtor does not follow the time lines, it can be very costly for the buyer. After the loan contingency removal date passes the buyer may be obligated to purchase the home by any means possible. If a problem occurs and the buyer is not able to obtain their loan after the contingency removal date, the seller can keep the buyers good faith deposit and may be able to sue the buyer for monies lost.

Extension of time: If at the end of the time frame period the buyer needs more time they can ask the seller for an extension of time. The seller can accept the extension and allow the buyer additional, or they can decide not to extend the extension and put the home back on the market and look for a different buyer and start the process over again.

DISCLOSURES

Disclosures are designed to inform the buyer of many different aspects including the home they are purchasing as well as the community and area they will be living in.

TDS: The sellers will fill out a TDS (transfer disclosure statement) that will notify the buyer of all things available in the home, any defects the home may have, and anything that may concern a new buyer when they purchase the home. It is very important the seller fill out the form completely to notify the buyer of everything about the home. The TDS will be given to the buyer to review and sign.

ZONE DISCLOSURE REPORT: The Zone Disclosure report will be ordered and given to the potential buyer. This report will notify the buyer of many required disclosures such as flood hazards, wildfire risks, geologic hazards, etc. Making sure the buyer is aware the home is in an earthquake or landslide area may save the seller from a lawsuit later down the road. This report is definitely designed to inform the buyer but is also very important in protecting the seller as well.

PRELIM AND HOA DOCS: The title company will process and provide with buyer with a preliminary title report to review. If the home has a homeowners association the title company will order HOA docs that will also be provided to the buyer to read and review.

MISC DISCLOSURES: Your real estate office may also provide additional city or county disclosures with local information. These disclosures are designed to advise the buyer of things they may not be aware of as well as protect the seller by providing the buyer all the information they can.

INSPECTIONS

As soon as the buyer and seller agree on a contract, inspections will be ordered. Many different types of inspections may be purchased by the buyer to make sure they know everything about the home they are trying to purchase. The buyer must first decide what inspections they want to purchase, a home, pool, roof, chimney, mold, well, septic, or any other inspection.

Sometimes after an inspection is received by the buyer, they may need to obtain additional inspections. If the home inspection shows that the air conditioner does not work you may need that to be inspected by an A/C specialists to decide if it can be fixed or if it needs to be replaced.

When the buyer receives the reports from the inspections they obtain, they might find something wrong with the home that was not previously known. When something is found in the reports, the buyer can either purchase the home as-is, they can ask the seller to help either with repairs or financial compensation, or they can choose not to purchase the home.

EXAMPLE: If an inspection found that tiles were missing from the roof the buyer may be concerned about damage that may happen when it rains again. The buyer may ask the seller to either have the tiles repaired before the close of escrow, or credit money to the buyer so they may repair it after they purchase the home.

APPRAISAL

The appraisal is a very important factor that can affect the sale of the home. An independent third party appraiser will need to assess the value of the property. This appraisal gives the bank lending the money on the property the assurance that the home is priced properly and that their investment in the home is correctly valued.

In some cases the appraisal of the home is lower than the purchase price offered from the buyer.

(1) The buyer can pay out of pocket the difference in the appraised value and the offered value.

(2) The seller can lower the purchase price of the home to the same value of the appraisal.

(3) If neither the buyer nor seller can/will pay the difference in price and the buyer will be unable to obtain their loan on the home. The buyer will need to cancel the purchase of the home and the seller will need to return the buyers good faith deposit and put the home back on the market for sale.

Both buyer and seller will want the appraisal done as soon as possible to ensure the value will be high enough to support the price offered to purchase the home.

ADDENDUMS

After the buyer looks at all the disclosures and views the inspection reports they may want to re-negotiate the terms of the contract. Any changes made to the contract after escrow begins will be done as an addendum to the contract.

Just as the negotiation of the purchase contract can go back and forth with many different options, the inspection/disclosure negotiation may do the same. The buyer may ask for several different repairs to be done to the home and the seller may agree to fix some items and not others. If no agreement can be reached, the buyer may decide to not purchase the home and the seller would need to give the good faith deposit back to the buyer and put the home back on the market.

Because the contract is renegotiated after inspections it is in everyone's best interest to complete the inspections as soon as possible.

ESCROW
STEP 3

INSURANCE

The buyer will need to obtain quotes from different insurance companies and decide what company they want to use to cover the home they are about to purchase. The Title Company and lender will need this information before the close of escrow.

BUYER AND SELLER SIGN DOCUMENTS

Approximately a week before the close of escrow the mortgage lender will provide the title company with loan documents. The title company will make arrangements for the buyer to sign all of the loan papers. These papers will need to be notarized and will most likely be signed at the title company office or at the buyer's home by a mobile notary. After the loan papers are signed, they will be returned to the mortgage lender. The lender will process the papers further and authorize the payment of the loan to the title company.

Around this same time frame the seller will need to sign papers as well. The seller's papers will be authorizing the title company to pay off the current mortgage loan on the home, sign the title of the home over to the buyers when they fund their loan, and advise the title company what to do with the seller's proceeds.

Any money due by either the buyer or the seller will need to be given to the title company at this time.

GOOD FAITH ESTIMATE / HUD-1

In the beginning of the escrow process the title company can supply you with a good faith estimate of bills, credits, and fees that can be expected. These estimates will show all fees paid out and credits given and how much money may be due or credited at the close of escrow.

At closing a HUD-1 will be provided that shows itemized charges imposed on the buyer and seller for the sale/purchase of the home. This form will show how much money the buyer/seller will need to pay or be receiving back as a credit.

LOAN FUNDING

When the title company processes the signed papers they return the loan packet back to the lender. The lender will process the loan packet and authorize funding to be sent to the title company.

DISBURSEMENT OF MONEY/RECORDING TITLE

The mortgage lender will fund the loan and money will be wire transferred to the title company. Once all the money is into the title company they will disburse funds. They will pay off the old liens on the home, pay all bills incurred during escrow, provide the seller any credits, etc.

The next business day the title company will record the deed with the county. When the deed is recorded the real estate transaction is complete and the new buyer can receive the keys to their new home.

NOTES

SECTION 5

GETTING READY TO MOVE

If you are hiring a moving company or moving yourself, it is important to be as organized as possible. Packing smart in the beginning can save you a lot of time and frustration during your move.

Moving is a very stressful and exciting time for everyone, make sure you concentrate on the exciting part, not the stressful part.

GET PREPARED

-If you are using a moving company, get a few estimates

-If you are moving yourself, you may need to get truck rental estimates or set up family and friends that may be able to help.

-Make arrangements for storage if necessary.

-Start a file for all moving paperwork, estimates and receipts.

-Set up things that need to be done at the new home: contact painters, carpet cleaners, roofers, etc.

-Return any borrowed items including library books, and retrieve any loaned items.

-Make sure you pick up your laundry.

-Purchase new door locks for the doors on your new home.

MOVING WITH CHILDREN

Depending on the age of your children, you may want to arrange for child care during the move. If your kids are older, they may love getting a task and helping to be a part of the moving process.

MOVING WITH PETS

It may also be difficult to care for your pets during your move and having a plan will ease some of your stress on moving day. Make arrangements to have a friend or family member care for pets, or reserve a spot at a local pet boarding shelter. After the move you can introduce your pets to the new home without people moving boxes in and out.

HOW TO PACK

Packing and moving can be very stressful; having everything in order can help ease some stress. Packing away items not used day to day, or seasonal items can be done during the escrow process. When the last papers are signed and keys are exchanged, the real fun will begin. Having everything organized can help you feel more at ease during the move.

- If you are using a moving company, it is a good idea to take a picture of valuable items before the move just in case you need to provide proof of damage later.

- Make sure you label all boxes well, but not too well. The boxes should tell the person moving them what room to put it in but not say what is inside the box so no one knows if valuables are inside. You can use a label system: the boxes should be labeled with the room it goes in and then also with a number. You can then have a paper that references the boxes that tells only you what is inside. Box kitchen2 has dishes, cups and bowls and box bedroom3 has towels, sheets and jewelry. Having an organized sheet telling you what is in each box will allow you to unpack boxes in the order you might need them.

- Use small boxes for heavier items and larger boxes for lighter items. If a box is heavy and large it is difficult to carry, but if the box is small and heavy it may be easier to pick up. Try to make sure all boxes weigh no more than 50 lbs. Any boxes over 50 lbs may be too heavy and awkward when trying to move and when unpacking.

- Having a separate box for all remote controls and electrical devices will be very helpful after the move.

- Leave some tools unpacked. You will have many items that will need to be taken apart to transport.

- Disassemble all items and furniture that need to be taken apart and save all the hardware in a labeled baggie. All assembly parts can be packed in one box so they will be easily found.

DON'T FOREGET ALL YOUR LOCAL RECORDS

MEDICAL

If you are moving to a new area be sure to gather copies of your medical records, x-rays, prescription information, etc. Don't forget your medical doctor, dentist, eye doctor, etc. Past medical records will be useful when a new doctor treats your family.

PERSCRIPTIONS

Make sure you fill all prescriptions before the move. You don't want to run out of medication while you are in transit. Try to transfer prescriptions before the move.

VETERINARY

Obtain all records from your veterinary clinic to give to your new vet. You can also ask your current vet for a recommendation of a new place in the area you are moving to.

CHILDREN'S SCHOOL RECORDS

It is important to inform your children's schools about the move and ask them to transfer their school records and transcripts to the new school.

TRANSFER SERVICE:

Disconnect service the day after you leave and connect service at your new location the day before you arrive to make sure you will have no interruptions. If you have any "last month" deposits make sure your request your refund.

PG&E, Water, Garbage

Telephone service

Cable

Gardener

Pest Company

Newspaper

Health club

Children's lessons

MAKE SURE YOU SEND ADDRESS CHANGES TO:

Family and friends

Post office

Auto registration/Insurance

Medical (Doctor, Dental, Optometry, etc)

Vet

Bank and credit card companies

Cell phone Company

Magazines

PACK A TRAVEL KIT:

Put aside critical items like:

Keys

Credit cards, money and ID

Important phone numbers and phone

Aspirin and medications

Toiletries

Flashlight

Paper towels

Paper plates

Cups

Travel alarm clock

Bandages

Games for the kids

Food for pets

Pack a suitcase with clothes and personal items

NOTES

GLOSSARY

Acceptance: A buyers and sellers mutual consent to enter into a contract with the agreed upon terms listed.

Agent: A person licensed by the state to conduct real estate transactions.

Application: A form used to apply for a mortgage loan.

Appraisal: A written analysis of the estimated value of a property prepared by a qualified appraiser.

Asset: Anything of monetary value that is owned by a person. Assets include real property, personal property, bank accounts, stocks, mutual funds, etc.

Breach: A violation of a legal obligation.

Broker: A person licensed by the state to conduct real estate transactions.

Certificate of title: A statement provided by a title company stating that the title to real estate is legally held by the current owner.

Clear title: A title that is free of liens or legal questions as to ownership of the property.

Closing: The buyer signs the mortgage documents and pays fees to finalize the sale of a property. The seller also signs final papers including forms that allow the title company to pay off the existing mortgage. Either party may have to bring cash to the title company at this time if funds are due to complete the sale/purchase of the home.

Closing costs: Expenses incurred by buyers and sellers in transferring ownership of a property. Closing costs normally include an origination fee, taxes, title insurance costs, etc.

Cloud on title: Any conditions revealed by a title search that adversely affect the title to real estate.

Commission: The fee charged by a broker for negotiating a real estate or loan transaction. A commission is generally a percentage of the price of the property or loan.

Commitment letter: A formal offer by a lender stating the terms under which it agrees to lend money to a home buyer.

Comparables: An abbreviation for "comparable properties." Comparables are properties like the property under consideration; they have reasonably the same size, location, and amenities and have been recently sold. Comparables help the appraiser determine the approximate fair market value of the subject property.

Comparative market analysis (CMA): An analysis of the current home for sale using comparables to figure the market value of the home.

Contingency: A condition specified in the purchase contract that must be met before a contract is legally binding.

Contingent offer: An offer made by a buyer on a home. The buyer will only purchase the home if their home sells first.

Contract: An agreement between two or more parties that creates or modifies an existing relationship.

Credit report: A report of an individual's credit history prepared by a credit bureau and used by a lender in determining a loan applicant's creditworthiness.

Debt: An amount one person owes to another.

Deed: The legal document conveying title to a property.

Deposit: A sum of money given to hold the sale of real estate.

Down Payment: The part of the purchase price of a property that the buyer pays in cash and does not finance with a mortgage.

Earnest money deposit: An amount of money paid by a potential buyer to show that they are serious about buying the home.

Equity: A homeowner's financial credit in a property. Equity is the difference between the fair market value of the property and the amount still owed on its mortgage. The amount of money a seller can make in profit when selling their home.

Escrow: Money and documents deposited with a third party to be delivered upon the fulfillment of a condition. The deposit of funds and documents by a Realtor to be disbursed upon the closing of a sale of real estate.

Escrow account: The account in which a mortgage server holds the borrower's escrow payments prior to paying property expenses.

Escrow disbursement: The use of escrow funds to pay real estate taxes, hazard insurance, mortgage insurance, and other property expenses as they become due.

Fair market value: The highest price that a buyer would pay and the lowest price a seller is willing to accept.

Fiduciary: The legal duty to act in the best interest of the beneficiary.

First mortgage: A mortgage that is the primary lien against the property.

Good faith deposit: An amount of money paid by a potential buyer to show that they are serious about buying the home.

Good faith estimate: An estimate prepared to advise the buyer or seller of fees, expenses, and credits incurred on the real estate transaction. Items that appear on this statement include real estate commissions, loan fees, points, taxes, HOA fees, etc. The totals at the bottom of this statement show the amount the seller will net from the sell and the amount the buyer is required to pay to complete the sell. This form is sometimes also called a HUD-1 statement.

Hazard insurance: Insurance coverage that compensates for physical damage to a property from fire, wind, vandalism, or other hazards.

Home inspection: A thorough inspection that evaluates the structural and mechanical condition of a property. A home inspection can be completed by a certified home inspector.

Homeowners' association (HOA): A nonprofit association that manages the common areas of a planned unit development or condominium project. Most HOA associations collect dues from the home owners to pay for community upkeep and expenses.

Homeowner's insurance: An insurance policy that combines personal liability insurance and hazard insurance coverage for a dwelling and its contents.

HUD-1 statement: An estimate prepared to advise the buyer or seller of fees, expenses, and credits incurred on the real estate transaction. Items that appear on this statement include real estate commissions, loan fees, points, taxes, HOA fees, etc. The totals at the bottom of this statement show the amount the seller will net from the sell and the amount the buyer is required to pay to complete the sell. This form is sometimes also called a good faith estimate.

Interest: The fee charged for borrowing money.

Interest rate: The rate of interest that will affect the monthly payment due.

Investment property: A property that is not occupied by the owner. The owner may choose to rent the property.

Joint tenancy: A form of co-ownership that gives each tenant equal interest and equal rights in the property, including the right of survivorship.

Liabilities: A person's financial obligations. Liabilities include any debts and fees owed to others.

Lien: A legal claim against a property that must be paid off when the property is sold.

Loan: A sum of borrowed money that is generally repaid with interest.

Loan origination: The process used by a mortgage lender to bring into existence a mortgage secured by real property.

Mortgage: A legal document that pledges a property to the lender as security for payment of a debt.

Mortgage broker: An individual or company that brings borrowers and lenders together for the purpose of loan origination. Mortgage brokers typically require a fee or commission for their services.

Point: A onetime charge by the lender for origination of a loan. A point is 1 percent of the amount of the mortgage.

Preliminary title report: The report on the title of a property from the public records.

Prepayment penalty: A fee that may be charged to a borrower, who pays off a loan before it is due.

Pre-qualification: The process of determining how much money a prospective home buyer will be eligible to borrow before he or she applies for a loan.

Principal balance: The outstanding balance of principal on a mortgage. This amount does not include interest or any other charges.

Principal, interest, taxes, and insurance (PITI): These four components are sometimes combined when making a monthly mortgage payment. Principal is the part of the monthly payment that reduces the remaining balance of the mortgage. Interest is the fee charged for borrowing money. Taxes and insurance is the amount that is paid into an escrow account each month for property taxes and hazard insurance.

Purchase agreement: A written contract signed by the buyer and seller stating the terms and conditions under which a property will be sold.

Real estate agent: A person licensed by the state to conduct real estate transactions.

Realtor: A designation for an agent or broker who is a member of the National Association of Realtors.

Rescission: The cancellation of a transaction or contract by the operation of a low or by mutual consent.

Recording: The noting in the registrar's office of the details of a properly executed legal document, such as a deed, a mortgage note, etc, thereby making it a part of the public record.

Title: A legal document showing a person's right to or ownership of a property.

Title Company: A company that specializes in examining and insuring titles to real estate.

Title insurance: Insurance that protects the lender (lender's policy) or the buyer (owner's policy) against loss arising from disputes over ownership of a property.

Transfer tax: State or local tax payable when title passes from one owner to another.

Underwriting: The process of evaluating a loan application to determine the risk involved for the lender. Underwriting involves an analysis of the borrower's creditworthiness and the quality of the property itself.

ABOUT THE AUTHOR

Kari Cross, grew up in a very close Portuguese family in Northern California. She has always cherished the close relationships with her family and enjoys giving that same care and attention to her clients.

As a local Realtor since 1998, Kari has assisted many clients buy and sell homes over the years. She enjoys helping her clients through the real estate process and creates long lasting relationships. Kari recognized that many people feel more comfortable when they know what to expect and know that things are going as planned. Clients that know each step of the process have a more pleasant experience from start to finish.

Kari is committed to help her clients before, during and after their real estate transaction. She gets much of her business from past clients repeat business and their confidence in her abilities to refer her to their friends and family.

This book was written by Kari as a tool to assist her clients, and other buyers and sellers, with information on the standard real estate process of buying or selling a home as well as important information about moving.

www.ingramcontent.com/pod-product-compliance
Lightning Source LLC
Chambersburg PA
CBHW072009060426
42446CB00042B/2277